Walt Disney's

DISNEYLAND

by Martin A. Sklar

THE BEHIND-THE-SCENES STORY OF HOW IT WAS DONE
. . . OF THE MAN WHO MADE IT POSSIBLE
. . . AND OF THE MILLIONS OF VISITORS WHO HAVE HELPED
MAKE IT THE HAPPIEST PLACE ON EARTH

Introduction

(Editor's Note: This introduction has appeared in each edition of **Walt Disney's Disneyland** since the book was first published in 1964. We continue to introduce the book in this manner because, perhaps more than any other single thing he did, Disneyland represents "the ideals, dreams and hard facts" of Walt Disney's own life and works.)

"To all who come to this happy place: welcome. Disneyland is your land. Here age relives fond memories of the past... and here youth may savor the challenge and promise of the future.

"Disneyland is dedicated to the ideals, the dreams and the hard facts which have created America... with the hope that it will be a source of joy and inspiration to all the world."

The spirit of Disneyland is embodied in these words, inscribed on the dedication plaque located at the base of the flagpole in Town Square on Main Street, where a visit to Disneyland begins. At the other end of Main Street is the Plaza, center of Disneyland; here, fanning out like the spokes of a wheel, the entrances to each of the Park's "lands" are located.

To walk from Town Square, down Main Street, and through each of these realms is to travel only a mile and a quarter. But that distance is measured not in steps or in hours; it is measured in personal experiences. Those who come to Disneyland call upon the whole spectrum of imagination to respond anew to those ideals, dreams and hard facts which are our heritage.

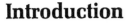

The Impossible is Fun

Lining the walls of WED Enterprises, where designers create new attractions for Disneyland, are sketches, plot plans and huge aerial photographs detailing the near and distant future. Here visitors, who often include international dignitaries, the world press, and representatives of American industry, preview what is to come at the Park. For years, art directors touring these guests past dreams that are to become realities, pointed to a map marked for expansion and casually, as though savoring some delicious private joke, explained: "And here, Walt's thinking about enlarging the Grand Canyon."

Like Disneyland itself, the humor has mellowed with age. Somewhere along the years, the quizzical, who-do-you-think-you're-kidding glances have disappeared. Today visitors simply nod in knowing appreciation. For no one but Walt Disney ever thought of recreating a Grand Canyon in the first place. And he did, in fact, enlarge it.

Walt Disney passed away in 1966. By then, his "dream" for a new kind of amusement enterprise had won international fame. *National Geographic* had seen it as a place "full of warmth and zest . . . where elephants really fly." *Time* magazine, calling Disneyland "California's No. 1 tourist attraction," had coined the term "the Disneyland Effect." A noted city planner rated Disneyland "the greatest piece of urban design in the United States today." And the ultimate flattery: during Walt Disney's lifetime, more than 60 million people visited Disneyland.

Among those visitors were 34 of the world's most famous citizens, including a dozen kings and queens and a baker's dozen presidents and prime ministers. Walt Disney personally escorted many of these dignitaries through Disneyland. "In a very meaningful, sincere manner," a State Department official recalls, "Walt sold America and Americana to foreign dignitaries. I have no doubt . . . that Walt Disney and Disneyland in a very real way have contributed to better understanding and a friendlier attitude on the part of world leaders toward the United States."

Yet from its very beginning, Disneyland was considered by many to be an "impossible" project, a "reckless gamble." How Disneyland grew from a persistent dream to a prodigious reality is the story in this book. That Disneyland succeeded is due to the man who had that dream. To Walt Disney, the impossible was always "kind of fun."

The Many Worlds of Disneyland

Disneyland is a "first"—an original. Since the day it opened in 1955, nearly 150 million people have come here from the earth's four corners to participate in adventures unique in all the world. Here, tomorrow is today, and yesterday is forever.

Disneyland is really many different worlds. It is 1890 again on Main Street, U.S.A. and 1980 in Tomorrowland. It is the pioneer's hardy worlds, Frontierland and Bear Country, and the grace and charm of a century ago just down the river in New Orleans Square. It is a jungle safari to far-off places in Adventureland. And it is a castle full of dreams—the classic tales of childhood "come to life" in Fantasyland.

Within the thematic realms of Disneyland are medieval castles and rocket ships of the future, horse-drawn streetcars and streamlined monorail trains, jungle elephants and elephants that fly, snowcapped mountains and colorful deserts. But Disneyland is much more.

What is Disneyland? It is the innocence of youth and the wisdom of age. It is a child examining the hitching posts that line an 1890 street and asking "Mommy, what kind of parking meters are these?" It is an elderly gentleman on the same street, smiling happily as he tells a bystander what he likes best about Disneyland: "I can jaywalk here." It is the children who telephone to ask, "Can I speak to Mickey Mouse?" and the telephone operators who answer, "I'm sorry, he's taking his nap now." It is a teenager aboard an 1850 stern-wheeler on a moonlit night, seeking an introduction to a girl by asking: "Is this your first trip abroad?" And it is an ambassador telling newsmen, "Disneyland is for kids . . . kids like you and me."

Disneyland is active participation in personal adventures that stimulate the imagination. A middle-aged lady about to "blast-off" into space suddenly leaves her rocket ship seat and rushes to the hostess, exclaiming: "I've got to get off—I'm afraid of getting air sick!" A little girl "submerged" aboard a submarine hears the captain announce that the vessel is "beneath the North Pole" and excitedly asks her daddy, "Will we see Santa Claus?" Thirty-five passengers turn their heads in unison as the "native guide" piloting a launch into the teeming jungles of

Disneyland is the sign in a glassware shop on Main Street, "Relax. We Don't Charge for Accidental Breakage," and another sign at Main Street's City Hall, "Lost Parents, Inquire Here for Children."

Disneyland is people forgetting their everyday cares and immersing themselves in the worlds of fantasy and adventure, yesterday and tomorrow — but no today. It is the late King Mohammed V of Morocco departing after an official visit, then eluding State Department escorts to see Disneyland a second time in an afternoon. It is the late President Eisenhower treating son John's youngsters to a day of fun like any other grandfather. It is Supreme Court Chief Justice Earl Warren dropping in unannounced late one afternoon "because everywhere I travel in the world people ask me about Disneyland." It is the Prime Minister of Pakistan, watching the old west show in Frontierland, receiving a direct hit from the comedian's water pistols — and laughing.

You find the magic of Disneyland in the soft pastel lighting of Sleeping Beauty Castle as evening approaches; in the twinkling eyes of a grandfather wearing an orange-billed Donald Duck hat; in a child kissing a life-like Mickey Mouse while Dad fumbles with his camera; in hard penny candy at the Market House; in kids following the band as it parades up Main Street playing a Sousa march; in secret passages in rock formations on Tom Sawyer Island — just big enough for kids to squeeze through, but far too small for a middle-aged spread.

Disneyland is the emotion that wells up within you when the *Mark Twain* stern-wheeler steams 'round the bend twinkling with pin lights from bow to stern, while nearby a Dixieland jazz band blasts out the classic "When the Saints Go Marching In." Disneyland is dozens of life-size Disney characters performing as they march and dance the length of Main Street in the annual Christmastime show, "Fantasy on Parade." It is teenagers dancing to the newest "rock" on a summer evening, while Mom and Dad turn over an old leaf to foxtrot and jitterbug and just listen to the time-honored sounds of the "big bands": Count Basie, Duke Ellington, Harry James, Benny Goodman, Louis Armstrong and many more have played here. Disneyland is fireworks bursting over a castle on a summer night, and the boastful Texan who claims, "Those were fine, but we have 'em bigger down where I come from." And the quiet lady standing next to him who smiles and asks, "Every night?"

But most of all, the spirit of Disneyland is found in the story of the boy who got his first real job at the age of 15, as a "news butcher" selling peanuts, candy, magazines and apples to people riding on trains

Adventureland, suggests, "Take a last look at the dock — you may never see it again!"

Disneyland is the complete absence of the tawdry "carney" barker. In his place is the smiling "Disneylander": the grey-haired man tugging on the reins of a powerful Percheron, pulling a trolley car down turn of the century Main Street; Pluto and Goofy and the Big Bad Wolf clowning for *your* camera and *your* children, even though there were thousands of other cameras and children already today; the pretty tour guide who admits she doesn't know the answer to your question, but promises to mail the information to your home — and does.

between Kansas City and Chicago. You sometimes saw him in the cab of an 1870 steam locomotive, taking its throttle for a grand circle tour around Disneyland. For Walt Disney loved to tinker—with old trains, and new ideas.

They Said It Couldn't Be Done

In the Minneapolis *Tribune* shortly after Disneyland opened, Will Jones wrote: "If it's an amusement park, it's the gosh-darnedest, most happily-inspired, most carefully-planned, most adventure-filled park ever conceived. No ride or concession in it is like anything in any other amusement park anywhere."

Disneyland, obviously, was never meant to be an "amusement park." The new concept in entertainment dedicated in Disneyland on July 17, 1955, was much more: a fabulous playground, something of a fair, a city from the Arabian Nights, a metropolis

of the future. Above all, it is a place for people to find happiness and knowledge.

When Disneyland opened in Anaheim (27 miles southeast of downtown Los Angeles), it was a 20-year dream come true for its creator, chief architect and head *imagineer*, Walt Disney. Rough drawings for a "Disneyland" had been found at the Disney studio dating back to the early 1930's, less than five years after Mickey Mouse made his film debut. "I was always trying to think of a place to take my two small daughters on a Saturday or Sunday afternoon—a place where I could have fun too," Walt told the *Reader's Digest*. "At an amusement park the only fun provided for a father, besides having his bottom dropped out from under him on the roller coaster, was the same he enjoyed all week: buying the tickets."

So Walt Disney began to dream, and to plan, a new kind of entertainment center for the young at heart of all ages. But the concept that emerged in the 1950's bore little resemblance to the small park Walt had first envisioned.

Members of his staff recall Walt talking about

building an intimate little park adjacent to his Burbank studio. It began as a "magical little park" two acres in size, with train and pony rodes, "singing waterfalls" and statues dedicated to the motion picture characters people throughout the world were already accepting as their own—Mickey Mouse, of course, and Donald Duck, Pluto, Goofy and the rest. It was to be a place to take visitors during tours of the studio and where studio employees might spend relaxing weekends with their families.

The concept never really took hold, however. For there is a basic truism that governs every success that bears the name Disney: no idea remains very long in its original form. Walt was a builder; his basic materials were ideas. He worked with them, played with them, grew with them, and finally—perhaps years after they first found expression—ideas emerged as tangible realities in motion pictures, television or Disneyland. (Today, the staff Walt Disney trained and worked with side-by-side for so many years, continues in the same manner. As Walt himself said, "We all think alike in the ultimate pattern.")

"It's as though Walt had a crystal ball," says a Disney executive. "If the bankers, or other people in show business didn't know what he was driving at, Walt just figured they didn't understand—and went right ahead with his newest idea because he personally believed in it. He was never off on 'cloud nine', yet he never did something merely because he thought it would be a commercial success. Every project had to be one that Walt himself felt would be fun to create."

Disneyland was one of those far-out ideas that few people other than Walt Disney believed in. One of those who had faith in the idea was Walt's older brother Roy, the business side of the Disney brothers since they founded the company in 1923. *Newsweek* once reported that "to build Disneyland Walt and Roy Disney borrowed to the corporate hilt, and then Walt sold his vacation home at a loss and borrowed against his personal life insurance policies."

Collectively, some of the more indifferent and reserved groups toward the concept of Disneyland were the nation's amusement park owners and operators. Early in 1954, four key members of the Disney staff assigned to develop ideas for Disneyland toured the major permanent amusement parks across America. Recalls one: "We could have paid for the trip with a few dollars from everyone who told us, 'If you don't put in a roller coaster and a Ferris wheel, you'll go broke.' Most were completely indifferent—especially the equipment manufacturers who had been building the same whips and shoot-the-chutes for years. They wanted us to buy what they already had, but

Walt had other plans. I can only remember two or three of the long-time amusement operators who offered any kind of encouragement at all."

It must have come as a shock to the amusement park men to hear that the baseball throw and the tunnel of love were to be relics of the past at Disneyland. And imagine a park without barkers; that was like planning a cinemascope *silent* movie.

In the final analysis, it was television which made Disneyland a reality. Just when all doors appeared to be closed, Walt Disney Productions and the American Broadcasting Company signed a seven-year contract that called for Walt Disney to produce a weekly one-hour television show. At the studio, its name had already been selected. The program would be called "Disneyland."

Disneyland, the television show, made its debut in the fall of 1954. Disneyland the park, built on sandy soil where 15,000 orange trees had grown, opened less than a year later.

There were many times during those 12 months of construction when the stumbling blocks had appeared insurmountable. One man recalls "tagging" the orange trees to be retained with strips of red paper and those to be removed with green. When a bulldozer operator began to fell the precious trees marked "save," it was discovered he was color-blind.

A construction supervisor remembers the blush of pride as water flowed into the Rivers of America in Frontierland for the first time . . . then the flush of desperation as the river promptly leaked its contents into the sandy soil of the former orange grove. Loads of clay soil had to be trucked in to waterproof the leaking river.

With the grand opening of Disneyland just two weeks away, more than 2,500 workmen were swarming over the land in two shifts that totaled 17 working hours a day. In this frantic setting, a television crew began positioning its cameras and rehearsing the scenes that would introduce Disneyland to America. The producer paled and hesitated as his gaze wandered over a scene where clouds of dust billowed and shifted as men and machines toiled. A Disney staff member stepped into the breach. "Don't worry," he comforted, "You'll have plenty of action to shoot. We'll be pouring cement!"

When Disneyland at last opened to an eagerly awaiting public, a mine train pulled out of its station in Frontierland, its load of contemporary pioneers comfortably seated in railway cars designed to recall those that once emerged brimming with silver ore from the mountain tunnels of the west. As the engineer headed his locomotive toward the buttes and

rock formations in the distance, he told a little story to his passengers: "A few years ago, this was all row after row of orange trees. Today . . . cactus, snakes, sagebrush, desert. That's *progress* for you!"

★　　★　　★

A Los Angeles newspaper, quoting an unidentified diplomat, recently reported: "All the crowned heads of Europe want to see Disneyland." Most of them already have—kings and queens, presidents, prime ministers, princes, princesses and even a few premiers —with one notable exception. By staying away, that exception splashed his name, and Disneyland's, across the front pages of newspapers around the world. His name: Nikita S. Khrushchev.

In September, 1960, Disneyland became the center of a *cause celebre* when the then-Soviet Premier startled millions of television viewers—and his American State Department escorts—by denouncing the evils of our capitalistic society in a novel way. It had, he said in effect, barred him from having a bit of fun because too many security precautions were necessary before he could visit Disneyland. The "international incident" set off quite a chain reaction:

● Author Herman Wouk wrote a letter: "I don't blame Khrushchev for jumping up and down in rage over missing Disneyland. There are few things more worth seeing in the United States, or indeed anywhere in the world."

● Bob Hope told a joke: "Here we are in Alaska, our 50th state. Alaska—that's halfway between Khrushchev and Disneyland."

● Mr. K. himself soon had an announcement: The Soviet Union, he said, planned to build a "country of miracles" park. Or, as the Moscow park would be called, "Miracleland."

● And in New York City the day following the

Soviet Premier's complaint heard 'round the world, an officer of one of capitalism's largest brokerage house telephoned a Disney executive. The Californian recalls the conversation:

"Maybe you don't remember me," the voice from the east coast said. "I'm the one who said we don't finance 'kiddylands' when you were looking for money to build Disneyland. Now I want to visit your place; if Khrushchev can get so mad over *not* seeing it, Disneyland can't be much of a kiddyland!"

Not an amusement park . . . certainly not a kiddyland. What then *was* the idea behind the creation of Disneyland? And who was qualified to design and shape this new medium of entertainment?

For the team that would help him build Disneyland, Walt Disney turned not to the experienced, skeptical amusement park operators. He turned instead to the field he knew best, motion pictures, and hand-picked a staff of artists, story tellers, machinists and special effects men unique not only for their skills . . . but for their wide-open eyes and minds.

At first consideration, the two mediums—indoor movies and outdoor entertainment—seem incompatible. But an art director who lived those hectic, formative days and nights has a ready explanation: "The basic premise in everything that went into Disneyland was participation, involving people in an experience, and—through that experience—evoking their emotions and stimulating their imaginations. Entertainment is basically an act of communicating with an audience, whether that audience is a theater full of people or a mother and daughter in a pirate galleon flying over Peter Pan's moonlit London town."

Several years ago, writing in the New York *Times,* Gladwin Hill described this accomplishment in similar terms: "What is the success of Disneyland? Many factors have entered into it. But to pin-point a single element, it would be imagination—not just imagination on the part of its impresarios, but their evocation of the imagination of the cash customers. Walt Disney and his associates have managed to generate, in the traditionally raucous and offtimes shoddy amusement park field, the same 'suspension of disbelief' which has been the secret of theatrical success down the corridors of time . . . In the theatre, the vital ingredient is not realism, but a blending of the real with the imaginary. The entertainer invites the audience to meet him half way. That is what has been successfully achieved at Disneyland."

Writer Ray Bradbury also perceived imagination at work and play in Disneyland. In a letter to the editor published in *The Nation,* Bradbury described his first

of many visits to Disneyland: ". . . I did better than take a child . . . I accompanied one of the great theatrical and creative minds of our time, Charles Laughton. I've never had such a day full of zest and high good humor. Mr. Laughton is no easy mark; he has a gimlet eye and searching mind. Yet *he* saw, and *I* found in Disneyland, vast reserves of imagination before untapped in our country."

Some have likened Disneyland to a gigantic stage, upon which each guest moves about—seldom a spectator, often an actor participating in the unfolding drama—an integral part of the humor, the pathos, the verve of a new "theatre."

And while Disneyland's basic appeal is to the Walter Mitty, the Admiral Byrd, the Sir Edmund Hillary and Jules Verne that lies dormant somewhere in the hopes and dreams of most of us, there is also the undertone of knowledge. Spoon-fed in the form of entertainment, the educational aspects of Disneyland seldom bubble openly to the surface. But they are always present, in the studied authenticity of a jungle safari, the recreation of frontiers both past and future, or the presentation of dozens of historic and science-factual adventures.

Added to the enormous task of blending all the ideas into a basic format for Disneyland was one more that posed the most difficult problem for its creators. Walt Disney wanted to design everything "new."

"Walt didn't want to build a new concept on old available ride machinery anyone could get his hands on," a designer recalls. "Almost everything we undertake has never been done before. Our unstated working axiom might be: *practice always works because it knows no theory*. If we dealt only in theory," he reasons, "many of Disneyland's most popular attractions would still be on the drawing boards."

For example, designers working on the projected Rainbow Caverns envisioned a series of underground chambers with dazzling ribbons of water cascading down the walls of the caverns and flowing in streams of red, green, blue and yellow throughout the caves. To check the practicality of the plan, the artists called in a noted scientist. His report was gloomy. He proved that within a week all the rainbow colors would be

Days of the buccaneers live again in
"The Pirates of the Caribbean."

the machine shop at the Disney studio. Piece by piece, each train was painstakingly designed and assembled. Finely detailed woodwork, metal and iron work and most parts were individually crafted right in the Disney machine shop. The two locomotives built for Disneyland in 1954-55 were a "diamond stack" and a "cap stack," both 4-4-0 engines (they have four wheels in front, four drive wheels, and no trailing truck or tender).

(There are now four trains on the railroad. One is pulled by a carefully restored 70-year-old locomotive that once hauled cane sugar on the Lafourete Raceland and Longport Railway in Louisiana. It was located for Disneyland by the Railroad and Locomotive Historical Society.)

Perhaps the most intriguing aspect in the design of Disneyland's trains was the manner in which scale was determined — and the resulting misconception, existing to this day, regarding the scale of buildings and other structures in Disneyland.

Walt's own *Lilly Belle,* ⅛ of full scale, was first "blown up" in drawings. Then a plywood "mock-up" was built, large enough for a man to walk through. When it was determined that a six foot door was adequate for a human passenger, the rest of the train followed in proportion. The size of the door dictated the size of the roof, the sides, and finally the wheels— 36 inches apart on the tracks, or almost exactly the same width as the narrow gauge railroads.

Standard railroad gauge is 56½ inches; Disneyland's 36-inch wheel spread is almost exactly ⅝ scale.

Popular notion is that all Disneyland is ⅝ scale. Actual fact is that only the trains, and some Disneyland vehicles such as the antique autos on Main Street, are ⅝ scale. Main Street itself is several different scales: 9/10 of full size on the first floors of its buildings, and a scale smaller — 8/10 at the second story level.

The Dream City

The real estate boom in a fantasy kingdom recently received a significant boost from a youngster in Peoria, Illinois. Scribbled the youth: "We are planning to move to Disneyland. Can you please send us some booklets about the rides and town?"

Many people have referred to Disneyland as a city unto itself. In a sense, Walt Disney's Magic Kingdom is a city . . . one with 6,000 "residents" (permanent and part-time employees) and more than nine million visitors each year.

but one — water-color gray. Walt listened to this dreary prediction, then turned to his associates and with a characteristic grin gave his own completely unscientific conclusion: "Well, it's kind of fun to do the impossible."

Six months later, the Rainbow Caverns opened at Disneyland. Today, years after their completion, visitors can pick out six distinct colors—and none of them is gray!

The "Lilly Belle" Grows Up

An engineer aboard the trains of the Disneyland Railroad reports that the thunder and lightning storm inside the Grand Canyon diorama has a great many passengers thinking it's for real. "Almost every trip," he reports, "I see five or six people poke their arms out of the train windows to see if it's really pouring."

Imagination again . . . but imagination born out of realism that begins the moment visitors step aboard the trains of the Disneyland Railroad. The detail and authenticity that characterize Disneyland may be said to take their cue from that railroad.

The *Lilly Belle,* a model train that once huffed and puffed around the back yard of Walt Disney's Holmby Hills home, was the prototype of the most letter-perfect 1890 railroad that ever whistled into a main street station. William McKinley and William Jennings Bryan on the campaign trail never had it better than the passengers taking a grand circle tour on the Disneyland Line.

In the months before Disneyland opened, two trains, an 1890 passenger and a western freight train, were constructed from the wheels and pistons up in

If Disneyland is to be called a city, it is one in which the major form of transportation is an imaginary "time machine." Whenever you step from this vehicle of the mind, you are in another age, another land—each one beckoning you to re-live the era, stories, hopes or dreams that it represents, and to participate in the varied entertainment within its own boundaries.

Today there are seven such individual "kingdoms" within Disneyland. But our story here begins at the beginning, describing the five original lands as they were during Disneyland's early years. Later, much of Disneyland's dramatic growth is detailed, as we show and tell about the two completely new lands and more than 30 new attractions that have sprouted in the former orange grove since opening day.

★   ★   ★

In the summer of 1954, construction began on this 160 acre "city" in Anaheim. A year later, when Disneyland opened its gates to the public, two million board feet of lumber and 5,000 cubic yards of concrete had gone into its construction, and one million square feet of asphalt had paved its streets and walkways. Giant earth-movers and bulldozers had moved 350,000 cubic yards of earth—enough to build a 20-foot high berm, one and one-eighth miles long around the entire place. "I don't want the public to see the real world they live in while they're in the park," Walt Disney observed. "I want them to feel they are in another world."

After nearly 20 years, the "magical little park" had become a $17,000,000 magic kingdom. The dream had at last come true.

Main Street, U.S.A.

You board Disneyland's "time machine" the moment you walk onto old Main Street, U.S.A. The contrast to the hustle and bustle of our modern world and its streamlined modes of transportation is sharp and penetrating. Suddenly, the entire mood changes, and the years roll backward—back to "anywhere in America," circa 1900. And *your* pace slows to match the leisurely clop-clop of the horse-drawn surrey, the um-pa-pa of a band concert in Town Square, the chug-chug of a horseless carriage.

Here once more is another age, rekindling fond memories or bringing to reality a page of Americana that previously existed only in a youngster's classroom history books.

"Many of us fondly remember our small home town and its friendly way of life at the turn of the century," said Walt Disney. "To me, the era represents an important part of our heritage, and thus we have endeavored to recapture those years on Main Street, U.S.A. at Disneyland. Main Street represents the typical small town of the early 1900's—the heartline of America."

An art director recalls the philosophy that governed design of this Main Street: "There is a subtle difference between the small towns and large towns of any era. For example, Disneyland's bank and opera house would be out of place in a large city; but in our small town, they are right at home. We were striving to get the most character and flavor into the creation of Main Street. It was much like doing a set for a motion picture. The story-value had to be brought out to put people back in the 1890-1910 period."

There is, however, a not-so-subtle difference between the buildings that line Main Street and a movie set. The latter is to be seen but not touched or entered by the audience; the former is a world of sights and sounds—plus the sensations of touch and smell and the personal adventure of examining, shopping and inhaling the nectar of nostalgia.

From the shelves of the old Market House filled with penny candy and fat, juicy pickles right out of the barrel, to the "white wing" whose shovel and receptacle were absolute essentials in an age when

horses were inviolate (but not necessarily sanitary), Disneyland's Main Street has been authentically re-created.

The design of Main Street is typical of the complete researching that has always been the springboard for a Disneyland attraction. Thousands of books, pictures and historical items were studied to get the feel of the interior and exterior of stores and shops of the 1900 era. A treasure hunt extended across the country into antique shops, private homes and out-of-the-way junk shops in small villages. The searchers tracked down relics of the past ranging from old lighting fixtures to the hitching posts of yesteryear.

What was found and brought back to Disneyland was the history of another age in bits and pieces. There were 100-year-old gas lamps from Baltimore and Philadelphia, grill work and railings from plantations in Nashville and Memphis, and small park benches from San Francisco.

This treasure contributes importantly to today's living of yesterday in Main Street's attractions, shops and exhibits: bank, book store, candle shop, market house, tobacconist, coffee house, ice cream parlor, photo display, registration and information center, china and glassware store, silhouette studio and City Hall. And, of course, the Cinema (silents only) where Rudolph Valentino is still "The Shiek" and hand-tinted slides graciously proclaim "Ladies Over 40 Need Not Remove Their Hats."

On Main Street, the horse and the "gasoline buggy," historic rivals, have become space age pals. Today teenagers laugh about "grandpa's hot rod" and call the horse-drawn streetcars "hay-burning oatsmobiles." But in a land where the skilled touch of the artisan is seen on every side, Main Street's vehicles are truly works of art—in mechanized form.

To re-create a fire engine that might once have answered the alarm in a small village of 1900 America, the designers sketched a chassis, then pored through standard catalogs for unlikely but practical equipment: a jeep rear axle, a three-speed truck transmission, the power plant of a small pickup truck, standard drive-line parts. To re-create a double-deck omnibus they used only *one* authentic part—an old electric Klaxon horn. The drop frame chassis is from a modern day truck, and the bus has both power steering and power brakes. To build-in a slight case of the shakes for the horseless carriage, the designers used today's most efficient two-cylinder water pump engine.

Main Street's old-time autos might delight visitors, but there was a very good chance they would scare the wits out of the ponies and Percherons who were to pull Disneyland's trolleys and surreys. So, in the weeks before the Park opened, the horses themselves were entertained. For four hours each day, they pranced around a circular ring while music, tooting automobile horns and the laughter and shouts of crowds blared at them from loudspeakers. Amid opening-day crowds, the animals felt right at home.

In an average year, Main Street's vehicles travel more than 23,000 miles, up and down the avenue. Their destination is the central Plaza—the stepping-off point for a journey into the many worlds of Disneyland.

Fantasyland

In medieval times, the drawbridge spanning a castle's moat was purely a defensive safeguard, cranked up to cut off an enemy's entry in time of attack. But when a castle with pink and blue parapets and towers became the entrance into the "happiest kingdom of them all," the drawbridge acquired a new meaning: it became the world's most unusual "welcome mat."

Beyond the drawbridge, in the broad courtyard of Sleeping Beauty Castle, classic stories of childhood are brought to life as adventures in participation for the young at heart. Some are outdoor attractions, for which the designers studied known principles of amusement park rides and adapted or completely revised them for new purposes. Others are Fantasyland's "dark rides," the indoor attractions in which black light, animation, sound and color effects are combined to create some of Disneyland's most beloved and beguiling entertainment.

Two decades of Disney motion picture entertainment provided the inspiration for the dark rides. From "Snow White and The Seven Dwarfs" came a trip through the Enchanted Forest and Diamond Mine. "Peter Pan" contributed a pirate galleon soaring high above the moonlit streets of London Town to Never-Never Land. Haughty caterpillar cars hurtle down the Rabbit Hole into the Upside Down Room, the Garden of Live Flowers, Tulgey Wood, and other settings from Alice's Wonderland. The "hot rodder" of storybook fable, J. Thaddeus (Mr.) Toad, emerges from "The Wind in the Willows" to topple barrels and frustrate policemen along the Road to Nowhere in Particular.

Fantasyland's outdoor attractions include the spinning, people-sized cups and saucers inspired by the Mad Hatter's tea party. Nearby, 72 steeds—70 to 90 years old and no two exactly alike—prance gaily to a calliope tune aboard the King Arthur Carousel,

largest of its kind in the world. And while the Casey Jr. Circus Train still "thinks he can" climb that steep hill, Dumbo continues to make history as the world's only elephant with aerodynamic ears.

(Long-time Disneylanders still shudder recalling the day a subcontractor delivered the first herd of Dumbos. Specifications called for the elephants to be light-weight "shells" so that the mechanism could lift pachyderm and two guests high into the Fantasyland air. The first ones were indeed "baby elephants"— each weighing 700 pounds!)

The Castle itself is a composite of many medieval palaces, though its designers were probably most influenced by a Bavarian fortress. Early drawings of the Disneyland Castle, in fact, looked so much like the German that the facade facing Main Street was extensively re-designed until today both Bavarian and French influences are present.

Though the Castle's tallest tower is but 77 feet above the moat, a device well-known in motion picture circles, forced perspective, has been used to trick the eye into telling the mind that the castle is much taller. The walls and battlements are constructed of stones cut in graduated sizes, from large ones at the foundation to small ones at the top-most sentry posts.

The same visual trickery has been used in Disneyland's tallest attraction, Matterhorn Mountain. A 1/100 scale replica of its Alpine namesake, Disneyland's "snow-capped" mountain is 145.6 feet high, but it appears much taller. Up, around and down its concrete and steel slopes (500 tons of structural steel, none exactly the same size) race four-passenger "bobsleds." Climax of a trip down the mountain is a splash into a pool of water at the base, thrilling the passengers—and stopping the bobsleds.

The mountain is pierced by a series of holes, through which the bobsleds race and trams of the Skyway glide on their airborne journey between Fantasyland and Tomorrowland. According to Disneyland legend, King Baudouin of Belgium is said to have asked Walt Disney why this Matterhorn has holes, and Disney is supposed to have answered, with perfect logic, "Because it's a Swiss mountain."

For perhaps the first time in history, landscapers were called upon to decide just exactly what constitutes "timberline" on a 14-story structure. Halfway to the Matterhorn's "snow-capped" summit, they decided, and planted varieties of pine ranging in height from 12 feet at the bottom to two feet at timberline. Forced perspective again.

From the biggest to the smallest in Disneyland is a journey of just a few steps—to Storybook Land. Here European canal boats and the Casey Jr. Train whisk you away to a "kingdom within a kingdom," where the delicate touch of the model maker and the landscaper's inventiveness combine to portray settings in miniature from Disney animated motion pictures.

Model makers at the Disney studio labored six months turning artists' visualizations of Pinocchio's Village, the straw-stick-brick homes of the Three Little Pigs, and other fable favorites into detailed buildings, on a scale of one inch to one foot. They made lead hinges so that six-inch doors would actually open for electricians to change light bulbs. They carved dozens of tiny toys for the window of Gepetto's shop. They installed minute drain pipes and hand-crafted "stained glass" and leaded windows.

Then the landscapers moved in, matching the miniature dwellings by ingenious use of plants and flowers. First they selected plants whose leaf-size was but one-quarter to one-half inch, then they restricted root growth by planting in containers. They met special design problems by pruning and shaping a three-foot tall Japanese boxwood, with gnarled trunk, to represent the oak tree where Alice entered the Rabbit Hole. They also uprooted a 100-year-old grape vine, turned it upside down and made it appear like the "terribly tortured old snag" in front of Ratty's home in "The Wind in the Willows."

The most difficult task was to locate *live trees that would not grow any more,* for the forest surrounding the home of the Seven Dwarfs. The answer to the problem seemed to be the Japanese *bonsai* tree. However, these tiny trees require constant care; poor trees were very expensive and good specimens were almost unobtainable. Near Mendocino, in northern California, the landscapers literally unearthed a much more perfect solution. Pine trees truly dwarfed in every respect were growing three to 12 feet in height in a "pygmy forest"—just 50 feet from the same species towering 60 to 80 feet tall! The dwarfed trees had rooted in a limestone shelf; their growth rate is so slow it is nearly impossible to measure. A dozen of these trees now "grow" in Storybook Land, in soil closely matching the nearly sterile conditions of that limestone shelf. Since planting at Disneyland in 1956, these trees have grown only about one inch per year.

Adventureland

"Walt Disney depleted our nurseries from Santa Barbara to San Diego," wrote Hedda Hopper on the eve of Disneyland's opening, and certainly no single project in memory taxed the commercial gardening trade as did Disneyland. Before construction began on the Park, the Disney acreage in Anaheim was almost entirely sandy-soiled orange groves. Today Disneyland is a botanical wonderland. Each year, 800,000 annual and perennial plants and flowers are planted and 1,000 trees transplanted to maintain springtime in the winter and showtime all year 'round.

Nowhere is the landscaping more vital than in Adventureland, where a unique combination of living plants and life-like animals has reproduced the atmosphere of the world's tropic regions, from darkest Africa to densest Amazon. Almost overnight, the banks of Adventureland's river were made to overflow with trees, flowers and grasses indigenous to the tropics. Fortunately, southern California is a sub-tropical region; nearly all the jungle plant life was available from major nurseries and private gardens within a 200 mile radius of Anaheim.

Among the most unusual plants growing in Adventureland today are the rare "Bushman's poison," which provides venom for the arrow tips of African hunters; the sacred Bo Tree of India; taro, staple diet of many tropic peoples; and giant bamboo growing as high as 50 feet. Today the biggest problem for Disneyland landscapers is the same encountered in any untamed land of dense vegetation: controlling the tangle of vines and ferns that grow in a true-to-life tropical jungle.

Adventureland's location within Disneyland was selected to take advantage of a row of eucalyptus trees used as a wind-break in the orange groves. Two tall, stately palm trees that once stood before the home of a pre-Disneyland orange grove owner, today blend into the tropic motif.

But Adventureland is more than trees and clinging vines. The Jungle River Cruise is a vicarious exploration for the stay-at-home dreamer, the adventurous spirit lurking somewhere in the hearts of all of us.

Many consider the Jungle River Cruise Disneyland's finest achievement. It compacts into a ten-minute experience the highlights, the *mystique* and excitement of a true-to-life adventure that could only be duplicated through weeks and months spent in the great outdoors. Source material for the designers was, in fact, gathered by photographers who did spend years in Africa—filming the Disney True-Life Adventure, "The African Lion."

Journey with 32 other passengers down tropic rivers, remote and mysterious, aboard bright canopied launches named for the world's waterways: *Mekong Maiden, Irrawaddy Woman, Ganges Gal.* Explore the misty rain-forest of the Amazon, the hippopotamus-filled waters of the Congo, the swirling rapids of the Nile. See a herd of elephants, "big shots and little

squirts," playfully spraying each other and "showering" under a waterfall. Watch the survival of the fittest in the grasslands filled with zebras and lions, jackals and giraffe. See the plight of the "trapped safari," chased up a tree by a snorting, short-tempered, nearsighted rhinoceros, while hyenas laugh their approval.

An Adventureland safari is nearly as wide-ear as wide-eye. For the "native guides" who pilot the boats keep up a constant stream of chatter, part rehearsed and part ad-libbed, but all in the true spirit of adventure and fun. "Please remove your earrings," they warn the ladies. "They attract the head-hunters." Or, "Keep your hands and arms inside the boat—these crocodiles are always looking for a hand-out." And, "Gentlemen, if your mother-in-law is still aboard, you've missed a golden opportunity."

It is the type of dialogue that could be as precarious as a real-life jungle excursion. That it succeeds is a tribute to that unique combination of living plants and life-like elephants, lions, hippos and gorillas—all members of a "cast" which has revolutionized entertainment. Adventureland, with its three-dimensional animated animals, was the proving ground where this revolution began.

In relative terms, it is a simple task to plan a mechanism for a special effect in a motion picture, one that will do the job once, twice or three times. But to design and build a machine that will produce the desired results and work reliably 12 or 14 hours every day—night and day—is quite another story. Mechanically, the animals are complex; at times, the maintenance crew has been known to rate the alligators "more trouble than real ones." Yet so life-like are the elephants, hippos and other animals who inhabit Disneyland's jungle that often, they startle Adventureland explorers with their realistic appearance and performance.

Seen from a front-row seat in a river packet, the Jungle River Cruise is tangible, personal adventure. Viewed from 70 feet above, the twisting waterway is serenity itself. The high vantage point is afforded by the largest of a rare, unnatural species of tree—the *Disneyodendron eximius,* an "out-of-the-ordinary Disney tree." Named for and designed after the Swiss Family Robinson's West Indies domain, its concrete roots penetrate 42 feet into the ground and 300,000 vinyl leaves "grow" on its many branches. Guests who climb to its top (stairs are thoughtfully provided) enjoy not only a wondrous view, but may tour the three-level Swiss Family Tree House, examining the furniture and fixtures used in the parents' room, the boys' room and the delightful open-air "parlor."

A second fantastic *Disneyodendron eximius* towers high above the Tahitian Terrace. The terrace itself is an extraordinary stage setting whose curtain is a cascade of water, and whose footlights are leaping flames of fire burning on the water. The highlight of summer evenings there comes when the falls magically draw aside, and from behind the waters sarong-clad natives appear to perform the swaying rhythms and rituals of the islands: the hypnotic barefoot fire walk, or the traditional grass-skirted dances of Samoa, Tahiti and Hawaii.

As they say in the travelogues, this too is Adventureland.

Frontierland

On a huge sound stage at the Disney studio in 1955, the era of Samuel Clemens' America was being reborn. For the first time in over half a century, a stern-wheel steamboat was being built in the United States: a triple-deck paddle wheeler, appropriately to be christened *Mark Twain.* Soon it would ply a muddy Mississippi of its own, but in the early stages of construction, the riverboat's greatest claim to fame was as real-life proof of an old joke about the man who built a boat in his basement—and couldn't get it out the door.

The *Mark Twain,* 105 feet long, 150 tons and designed to carry 350 passengers, was indeed too big to move through the doors of even the giant sound stage—in its entirety. But this "queen of the river" was rather an unusual vessel: it was the first ever prefabricated stern-wheeler—built in sections to be dismantled, trucked over freeways piece by piece, and reassembled at Disneyland!

Much of America's history is the story of frontiers awaiting conquest. To Walt Disney, a keen student of history, Disneyland could not be complete unless it told the story of America's pioneer development. As Walt had said, "All of us, whether tenth generation or naturalized Americans, have cause to be proud of our country's history, shaped by the pioneering spirit of our forefathers. It is to those hardy pioneers, men and women of vision, faith and courage, that we have dedicated Frontierland."

Disneyland's frontier stretches from the 1790's to the 1870's, and within the log stockade that serves as its entrance, touches on some of the most colorful aspects of American pioneer history: the boisterous frontier of Davy Crockett, the southwest with its rollicking dance halls, the charm and elegance of southern plantations, the captivating lure of the ghost

towns, and the romance of Tom Sawyer's Mississippi.

Like many a frontier town a century ago, Frontierland is built along a river, the half-mile long "Rivers of America." It was for travel on this waterway that the *Mark Twain* was created. Today, literally, the river is one of the world's busiest.

Here sails the *Columbia,* exact full-size replica of the first American ship to circumnavigate the globe (1787-1790). Built in Disneyland's own dry dock, this full-rigged, three-masted ship is the first such vessel constructed since the Civil War. It is a marvel of precise craftsmanship, right down to its "dead-eyes" and to the cotton and tar oakum used in hand-caulking its decks.

Here cruise the Mike Fink keelboats and Davy Crockett's explorer canoes—both authentic reproductions of the smaller craft that once navigated the inland waterways of America. The canoes furnish Disneyland's most active participation: personal paddling.

Here log rafts float from the mainland to another world—Tom Sawyer Island. Located in the middle of the River, the Island is a youngster's paradise, offering an adventure from the pen of Samuel Clemens. There's a bridge made of barrels and a suspended one that sways. There's old Fort Wilderness, and a huge rock that teeters like a seesaw. And there's the dark, mysterious Injun Joe's Cave.

Bordering the river is a composite True-Life Adventure, based on elements of four Disney films, three of them Academy-Award winners. "Beaver Valley," "Bear Country," "The Living Desert" and "The Olympic Elk" provided the inspiration for this seven-acre attraction called Nature's Wonderland. So realistic are the 200 life-like animals, birds and reptiles that the migratory birds which fly over Disneyland have often attacked the animated ravens and owls. With its forest, desert and mountains, with "Old Unfaithful Geyser" spouting water 70 feet in the air, and with its colorful Rainbow Caverns, Nature's Wonderland is indeed the early western wilderness, re-born for a later western civilization.

Tomorrowland

Reactions of Russian visitors to Disneyland have always been closely followed by American communications media. Photographers covering the tour of the Moscow Symphony Orchestra in 1957 were anxious to obtain a picture of the Soviets near the *Rocket to the Moon,* conveying their request through an interpreter. Animated discussion among the Russians followed, then a chorus of laughter and the interpreter's return. "They want to know," he dead-panned, "whether Walt Disney will guarantee the return trip."

Several years ago, in *Ford Times* magazine, Art Linkletter wrote: "On my House Party show, I frequently ask the kids if they've been to Disneyland, and if so, what they like best. One youngster told me, 'I like the scary rides, like the Matterhorn Bobsled Run; but Daddy always takes me on the submarines —he likes the mermaids!' "

These stories tell a tale of Tomorrowland: here factual science lives, but tongue-in-cheek sometimes tiptoes close behind.

Originally, Tomorrowland's goal was to present "a living blueprint of our future." Of all Disneyland's realms, Tomorrowland was the most difficult to conceive and design, and it has undergone the most change. For Walt Disney and his artists were working not in the devil-may-care world of science fiction, but in one based upon conceptions of tomorrow held by some of America's foremost men of science and industry. And in the world we live in, what is tomorrow *today* is seldom tomorrow *tomorrow.*

"Lasers," "fly-bys," "communications satellites"— such terms and the technology to achieve them were unknown in 1954, when Tomorrowland was originally designed. Even the household word "astronaut" was still to be coined. That Tomorrowland was a success with Disneyland guests is in large part due to the experts who acted as advisors in the precarious business of predicting.

When Walt Disney determined Tomorrowland must have a science-factual flight to the moon, he enlisted two of America's outstanding authorities as the stargazers: Dr. Werner Von Braun, then chief of the U.S. Guided Missile Development Division; and Willy Ley, space travel expert.

Several years earlier, in a national magazine article, they had predicted the moon *could* be reached in ten years. Disneyland's simulated space flight, however, was not conceived as a space voyage of one or two astronauts, but rather a scheduled flight that blasts off at regular intervals, circles the lunar body without landing, and then returns to the safe harbor of Disneyland's Spaceport.

Von Braun and Ley projected such flights could be routine by 1980. Taking the basic data they supplied, the Disney staff applied all the skills of motion picture special effects to create the proper moon-scape and in-flight views. Five years later their task would have been immeasurably more simple; in 1954, no film of actual blast-off was available, nor was there photography of the Earth from satellites in space. Every facet of the trip had to be realistically simulated.

Today, engulfed in the sounds of rocket blast-off and gently shaken by seat vibrations simulating take-off, landing and weightlessness, space travelers participate in the early realization of one tomorrow. So accurate were the original predictions that the astounding events of actual space exploration required —in the first dozen years—only the addition of orbiting satellites to make the prophecy and man's accomplishments correspond.

In Tomorrowland the far reaches of outer space are but moments away from the distant depths of liquid space. On the Submarine Voyage, on a typical Disneyland day, thousands of visitors pass within touching distance of 24-karat gold valued at thousands of dollars. But the treasure in glittering urns and trinkets has its own built-in safeguards: first, it is under ten feet of water and second, it is protected by sharks, octopi, electric eels and even a sea serpent.

The gold is on view in the Submarine Voyage, a $2,500,000 journey to the bottom of the sea, where neophyte mariners chart a course aboard the grey-hulled vessels of, numerically, one of the world's largest undersea fleets. Disneyland's submarines, scale versions of America's nuclear-powered navy, sail daily through a South Seas coral lagoon, beneath the Polar Ice Cap, through an underwater earthquake in the Lost Continent of Atlantis, past barnacle-laden Venetian galleys in the graveyard of sunken ships, and into a mermaid lagoon.

To enjoy the vast wonderworld at the bottom of

the sea, each of 38 submarine passengers has his own individual porthole. Nearby, to preview the future of mass rapid transit, 127 seated passengers travel at speeds up to 45 miles per hour aboard trains of the Disneyland-Alweg Monorail System.

Early in the planning for Disneyland, Walt Disney expressed interest in a "train of the future" for Tomorrowland. In 1957, following a visit to Cologne, Germany, the engineering staff recommended a design that appeared to offer the best prospects for economy, stability and all-around practicability, not only for Disneyland but for municipal transportation in general. Within two years Disneyland had become the first "city" in America to introduce a passenger-carrying monorail operating on a daily schedule.

Electrically powered, running on rubber tires over a concrete beamway, a *highway in the sky,* these almost silent trains immediately captured the public's fancy. Within two years the entire system was extended outside Disneyland for a practical transportation purpose: carrying passengers between the Disneyland Hotel and Tomorrowland's station.

Today the Disneyland-Alweg Monorail System is two and a half miles long, parallels a major highway and crosses a city street. Basic design of its three trains, including power, brake and safety systems, could easily be used in metropolitan transit.

Monorail is a very old idea, not a new phenomenon. Since 1901 Wuppertal, Germany, has had a suspended monorail in which cars ride under the beam — in contrast to the straddling, piggy-back style of Disneyland's. But in an age when urban transit problems are "cussed and discussed" almost daily, Walt Disney was pioneering once again with a showcase for public examination and enjoyment. As an executive of a major transportation company said later, "You've built this entire system in less time, and for about the same money, that my company would allocate for a *feasibility* study!

How has Tomorrowland, that "living blueprint of our future," fared in practice? In some ways, quite successfully. For one, it has proved to be an ideal framework for displays by American industry. Over the years, Monsanto has demonstrated a potential new dimension for plastics in home construction; the Bell System has used Disneyland for the first major public demonstrations of the picture phone and the family phone booth; and the McDonnell Douglas moon flight has contributed to public understanding of distant space travel, while at the same time "keeping up with the times" — in 1975, thanks to Mariner 9 and NASA scientists, it became the *"Mission to Mars."*

Tomorrowland has showcased several important new developments. The piggyback type monorail, for example, may have an unlimited metropolitan future. As writer Robert DeRoos said in *National Geographic,* "Most passengers, myself included, leave the monorail convinced it is the answer for rapid transit of the future."

Circle-Vision, the 360-degree motion picture technique premiered at Disneyland in 1955, has already contributed to an understanding of the U.S. through showings of *America the Beautiful* at the Brussels World's Fair, a United States exhibit in Moscow, and other major expositions. The audience watches its encircling film from the center of the action so that they may see, almost simultaneously, in front of them and behind them, and all the scenery in between.

Even the narrow ribbons of roads which make up Autopia's freeways, with multi-levels, criss-crosses and divided one-way lanes, were a prediction of things to come in 1955. Few states in America had an ultra-modern expressway system to match Disneyland's in those days.

Experts on road construction and safety no doubt found Autopia interesting in the early years. Over the years, however, it is the student of human nature who has been most intrigued by this miniature turnpike system. For side by side with youngsters gaining their first experience behind the wheel of a real auto, the same adults who grumble and fume about traffic on southern California's full-size freeways plunge happily into Autopia's junior size traffic jams in scaled-down sports cars. Obviously, tomorrow can be a wonderful age.

"Disneyland Will Never Be Completed"

When Disneyland opened, Walt Disney told a nationwide television audience, "Disneyland will never be completed. It will continue to grow, to add new things, as long as there is imagination left in the world."

Even as the first visitors poured into the Park, Walt Disney was planning for the future. "Walt had the daring, the audacity, to stake his personal reputation on something he believed in — and to visualize what it would be like when completed," observes a close associate. "Other people would have said, 'We have spent $17 million and we sure hope it's successful so we can get our money back.' But Walt was saying, 'It cost $17 million, people will have fun, and next year we'll add . . .' "

"Next year we'll add . . . " No single phrase more clearly sums up the story of Disneyland since its debut. By the 1970's, the park that was "something of a fair, a city from the Arabian nights" had become a $125-million international playground visited by citizens of more than 100 nations, and annually attracting more than nine million patrons, over six million of them adults. Originally it had 22 attractions; today there are more than 50.

The First Decade

The story of Disneyland may be divided into several distinct periods. The first decade was highlighted by the establishment and public acceptance of Disneyland—a brand new concept in the arena of family entertainment. The second decade, which began in 1965, was marked by unprecedented expansion in the style and variety of attractions, and in the number of visitors. The third decade began as Disneyland celebrated its 20th Birthday in July, 1975.

Few people, as Disneyland approached its opening in July of 1955, looked upon it as a concept that would prove successful. But Walt Disney had faith in his idea. "I think what I want Disneyland to be most of all," he said, "is a happy place—a place where adults and children can experience together some of the wonder of life, of adventure, and feel better because of it. (Disneyland) has that *thing* — the imagination, and the feeling of happy excitement, I knew when I was a kid."

There were physical additions to Disneyland in its first decade, of course. In one year alone, the monorail, the Matterhorn, the Submarine Voyage, a second Autopia freeway system, and a new motor boat cruise were added to the Park's list of major attractions, dramatically changing both Tomorrowland and Fantasyland.

But more significantly, the dynamics of Disneyland's first decade were provided by new ideas that were tried within the new concept itself. Some—like a circus every day and other special "days" for local-area residents—were introduced and soon discarded with little success. Others—like the traditional parades, special one-night entertainment events, and especially new kinds of shows made possible by space-age advancements in the animated arts—were popular successes from the day they were introduced. Many continue to this day.

A look at one of the major ideas that failed, and several that succeeded, illustrate the special way in which the public quickly came to look at Disneyland.

In November and December, 1955, Disneyland introduced the "Mickey Mouse Club Circus." Six weeks or so prior to its debut, the *Mickey Mouse Club* television show had swept the country with its

Birds talk and flowers croon in the Enchanted Tiki Room.

boundless enthusiasm and entertainment for young people. The Mouseketeers — Cubby, Darlene, Bobby and especially Annette — became household names and faces. No daytime program for children has had its impact, before or since.

The "Mickey Mouse Club Circus" seemed a natural. Under the big top, the Mouseketeers would make their first public appearance, supported by 12 major acts featuring 80 animals and 70 performers. It was a 75-minute extravaganza inside the world's only heated circus tent. Best of all, admission was just 50 cents.

The circus, however, lasted just one season at Disneyland. Despite the popularity of its stars, and the quality of the show itself, attendance results were disappointing. Today the reasons seem clear. People come to Disneyland to race down the Matterhorn in a bobsled, explore pioneer America aboard stern-wheeler or sailing ship, and cruise down the jungle rivers of Adventureland. These and many more are experiences unique to Disneyland; taken together, they are reasons for traveling thousands of miles to see Disneyland, as so many do. But the circus, Mickey Mouse Club or not, is still a traveling act. In various sizes, it comes into towns across the U.S.A. once or twice or three times every year. Unlike almost all the entertainment Disneyland presents, a circus was not *unique* to the Magic Kingdom.

What *is* unique in the arena of special events are the nighttime shows developed specifically for Disneyland. By their very nature, they exist only because of Disneyland. Without the Park's thematic settings, and especially without Disneyland's own attractions as part of the show, these special parties could not take place.

Names and numbers tell the tale of their popularity. Twenty thousand guests attend the world's biggest New Year's Eve Party (serving soft drinks only). More than 100,000 teenagers from 550 schools as far away as Hawaii, Utah and Nevada attend one of seven "Grad Nights" for high school seniors (the event is so popular there's a waiting list of schools that want to attend, and more than 5,000 graduates arrive by plane from distant cities). A "Big Band Night" featured the likes of Ellington and Basie, and Louis Armstrong often headlined "Dixieland at Disneyland." Favorites of the young are featured at the annual Valentine Party, the Spring Fling and other special nights throughout the year.

These events are an outgrowth of Disneyland's nightly entertainment line-up during the summer months. Shortly after nine each evening, and every summer evening since 1957, the *Fantasy in the Sky* fireworks burst over Sleeping Beauty Castle, signaling the start of southern California's most diverse night life. Dance bands swing out with the electric rhythms of the teens, the foxtrot for dads and moms, two-beat Dixieland, and even the swaying melodies of Pacific Islands. Over the years, the hootenanny has found a home here, and the rousing spirituals of gospel choirs, and all the myriad twists and turns of the ever-changing rock generations.

While special entertainment and big name stars often enjoy the headlines, it still remains that as the first decade drew to a close, a new star whose roots grew in the space age had become the biggest every day attraction at Disneyland. Upon its electronic commands, hundreds of performers have "come to life."

Like many another headliner spawned in the entertainment capitals of the world, its name is a composite description of its talents. *Audio-Animatronics* is the word coined to describe the ingenious electronic system that animates the performers of so many latter-day Disneyland shows.

In simplest terms, *Audio-Animatronics* combines and synchronizes sound and animation with the electronics of the space age. Disney technicians devised complex ways to "program" movements, sound, music and dialogue and record them on tape. Hundreds of separate actions can be programmed in sequence and stored on tape. When the tape is played back, elec-

"The Walt Disney Story", at the Opera House on Main Street, recalls half a century of Disney entertainment, from Mickey Mouse to the Magic Kingdoms of Disneyland and Walt Disney World in Florida. A highlight is the tracing of Walt Disney's development of the "art of animation", from simple one-reel cartoons to the complex three-dimensional Audio-Animatronics shows. Climax is the theatre performance of "Great Moments with Mr. Lincoln."

tronic impulses activate air cylinders, pistons, springs and valves inside the "performers." Magically, birds talk in the Enchanted Tiki Room, a bearded sea captain swings his sword in the Pirates of the Caribbean, and little girls dance the cancan in It's A Small World.

Audio-Animatronics made its debut in 1963 in the Enchanted Tiki Room, a theatre show where 225 birds, flowers and tropic tiki idols sing and joke and chant. The show is one surprise overlapping another; first the birds "come to life," then the flowers join in a musical luau and finally — with accenting claps of thunder and flashes of lightning — a tropical storm bursts through the Tiki Room.

Many have written about *Audio-Animatronics* and the Enchanted Tiki Room, but few have caught its spirit, and Disneyland's, as did Dr. Don D. Jackson. Writing, of all places, in *Medical Opinion & Review,* Dr. Jackson marveled: "There was the timing — the incredible circuitry that surprised and never faltered. There was the mystery; the 'how could it be, how in the world did they manage to . . . ?' Above all, there was a creative presence, an aura of wonderment that inevitably surrounds the results of a spectacular human collaboration — from a child's birth to a symphony."

"As do many creative people," appraised Dr. Jackson, "(Walt) Disney enacted the hope and idealism of modern-day innocence — the persistent belief, in the face of overwhelming technological reasons for why 'it can't be done', that men can achieve whatever they can conceive."

The Second Decade

As Disneyland's first decade drew to a close, an event 3,000 miles away was about to change the entire landscape of the Park. In retrospect, it may be seen that the New York World's Fair 1964-65 was to exert perhaps the most important single influence on the future of Disneyland.

For two springs and summers at the World's Fair, new Disney entertainments had captivated eastern audiences. Ninety-one percent of the Fair's paid attendance — 46,871,236 people — visited the four attractions Walt Disney and his staff had created. Like the story of Disneyland itself, the story of Disney-at-the-Fair also revolved around the design studios of WED Enterprises. There, often side-by-side with new ideas for Disneyland, the World's Fair attractions for General Electric, Pepsi-Cola, Ford and the State of Illinois were conceived and designed. Each was a show in the Disneyland tradition.

By the time the World's Fair had ended in October, 1965, plans were already well advanced for these four shows to return to California and Disneyland. One, General Electric's "Carousel of Progress," became the catalyst for rebuilding the entire Tomorrowland area in 1967. Two others — It's A Small World and the Primeval World of the dinosaurs — returned to Disneyland as part of the expansion of existing areas and attractions in 1966. The fourth, Great Moments with Mr. Lincoln, had already opened at Disneyland in the summer of 1965, before the Fair had even closed its gates.

As Walt Disney wrote in commemorating Disneyland's tenth anniversary. "Now we are embarking on our second decade, and it promises to be even more exciting than the first. In fact, we are already creating and designing new attractions for almost every year in the next ten." It was "next year we'll add" all over again.

While the World's Fair shows were the cornerstone of this growth, the idea for at least one had really begun even before Disneyland celebrated its *first* birthday. Walt Disney had long held the belief, shared by many Americans, that more of us should recognize the influence of historical events on our lives today . . . and the significance of our American heritage in the future development of this nation. That belief was the motivation for *Great Moments with Mr. Lincoln.*

Ten years of research and thousands of man-hours by artists, sculptors and skilled technicians — experts in the new art of *Audio-Animatronics* — went into the creation of an incredibly lifelike figure of America's sixteenth president. When "Mr. Lincoln" rises from his chair to address Disneyland audiences, the words are those of the Great Emancipator, words as applicable today as they were a century ago:

"What constitutes the bulwark of our liberty and independence?" asks Mr. Lincoln rhetorically. "It is not our frowning battlements, our bristling sea coasts. These are not our reliance against tyranny. Our reliance is in the love of liberty which God has planted in our bosoms. Our defense is in the preservation of the spirit which prizes liberty as the heritage of all men, in all lands, everywhere. Destroy this spirit, and you have planted the seed of despotism around your own doors."

"Let us have faith," Mr. Lincoln counsels, "that right makes might, and in that faith, let us, to the end, dare to do our duty as we understand it."

(In 1975, a decade after *Great Moments with Mr. Lincoln* was first performed at Disneyland, it became the highlight in the story of Walt Disney's "art of animation." In *The Walt Disney Story* at the Main Street Opera House, visitors follow the birth and growth of Disney animation, climaxed by the three-dimensional performance of the dramatic Lincoln show.)

History of a vastly different sort, some of it predating man on earth, provided the themes for two of Disneyland's major attractions in the $20 million expansion of 1966. One is the *Primeval World*.

Boarding trains of the Disneyland Railroad, guests first travel through the Grand Canyon diorama, then are whisked back in time many millions of years to a day when giant creatures thundered over the land or soared like gliders across the sky. In the Primeval World, brontosaurus, stegosaurus, pterodactyl, triceratops and the frightening king of all the dinosaurs, tyrannosaurus, "come to life" again through Audio-Animatronics.

These giant reptiles, ranging in height up to 15 feet, actually roamed the North American continent ages ago. In Disneyland, both the vegetarian brontosaurus and carnivorous tyrannosaurus, life-size and life-like, once more rule an earth changing from misty swampland to fiery, erupting volcanoes.

New Orleans Square

Historical fact and a dash of dashing fable also influenced Walt Disney and the WED staff in the creation of an entire new land, *New Orleans Square*, and its major adventure, *Pirates of the Caribbean*.

Several years before the opening of New Orleans Square, the *Yale Architectural Digest* described Disneyland in words that, perhaps, are more appropriate to New Orleans Square than to any other area of the park:

"By almost any conceivable method of evaluation

that does not exclude the public, Disneyland must be regarded as the most important single piece of construction in the West in the past several decades ... The skill demonstrated here in recalling with thrilling accuracy all sorts of other times and places is of course one which has been developing in Hollywood through this century. Disney's experts are breathtakingly precise ... "

In both atmosphere and architecture, New Orleans Square recreates the Crescent City in its golden age a century ago. Along its winding streets and in sheltered courtyards are Disneyland's most distinctive adventures in shopping and dining. Literally years of research and study went into the planning; out of this attention to detail and desire to recreate the classic traditions of old New Orleans came a series of "showcases." Here, in a land as large as Main Street, each

shop and restaurant is one "act" in a thematic adventure; each dramatizes — in sight, in sound, and in antique merchandise—one part of the exciting legend that was New Orleans, vintage 1850.

There is *Mlle. Antoinette's Parfumerie,* where ladies may scent and sample perfumes in a setting where elegant mirrors revive the lost art of painting "in reverse" (a decorative process in which the mirrors were silvered only after the artist completed her painstaking work). *The Café Orléans* is distinguished by its tile floor and zinc-top coffee bar; espresso is served here from an ancient steam machine admired and purchased by Walt Disney in Milan, Italy. *Le Gourmet* offers hard-to-find culinary accessories. The brick-walled *French Market* attracts diners with two tile murals depicting early New Orleans, while *The-One-Of-A-Kind Shop* displays antiques for sale ranging in

By Thomas Nebbia ©National Geographic Society

value to thousands of dollars. Nearby, the exciting *Blue Bayou Restaurant* serves *poulet, crevettes, boeuf* and *poisson* by candlelight, which is only proper in a setting where moonlight shines all day long and the sight of the bayou at night creates a mood at once mysterious and adventurous.

To find adventure of a totally different kind in New Orleans Square is to walk along Royal St., down Front St. into Pirate Alley. There, at the end of the quay, flat-bottom *bateux* take on their seafaring guests, then glide serenely across the Blue Bayou Lagoon. Suddenly the boats plunge down a steep waterfall into the lair of the *Pirates of the Caribbean.*

In its four-page story, "Anyone for Yo-ho-ho?", *Life* Magazine told of the daring adventure and how it came about. "In the costliest and most technologically sophisticated amusement park ride ever built, California's Disneyland has evoked the blood-curdling buccaneering past of the Spanish Main. Called *The Pirates of the Caribbean,* it is a 15-minute boat ride through the sacking of a town, marked by as harrowing a series of misadventures as the likes of Captain Kidd and Jean Lafitte ever visited upon the hapless victims . . .

"It was some years ago," *Life* continued, "that (Walt) Disney put his artists and engineers — his "Imagineers" as he called them — to work on his idea for a boat ride through a pirate-vs.-townspeople display . . . The Imagineers went back to work, drawing upon space and computer-age technology to try to create human and animal facsimile that would move. As the Imagineers got better and better results from their new science of *Audio-Animatronics,* more and more experimental models began to show up in other Disneyland displays . . .

"The complicated movements . . . are programmed into computers that are slightly modified versions of the ones used by the National Aeronautics and Space Administration. With a precision that would do credit to a moon shot, these coordinate everything that transpires during the sacking and burning of the village — and none of the Audio-Animatrons ever misses a cue.

"Great attention has been paid to detail. For example, one drunken pirate sits on a pier, happily playing his picolo, his fingers running over the little holes in the instrument as his cheeks puff out at the proper moments. If you were to duplicate his finger movements while blowing on an actual picolo, you would play the same ditty, note for note . . .

"At another point the boat gets caught in a cross fire that starts when a pirate aims a cannon and lets fly. When the pirate cranes his neck to see if he's on target, the 20 people in the boat do the same, just as the cannonball supposedly hits a building and sets it afire. In the answering volleys it is all the customers can do to keep from cringing on the floor of the boat."

Small wonder, then, that The Pirates of the Caribbean has become Disneyland's single most popular and successful adventure. For as *Life* pointed out, its mechanized cast — 64 human figures and 55 animals — represents a kind of artistic and scientific masterwork for the *Audio-Animatronics* process. The pirates themselves are the end product of what *Life* called "the complicated steps in their evolution from the old-fashioned wax-works-type display they once inhabited."

*   *   *   *

Another small wonder new to Disneyland in 1966 awaits visitors who board other boats on the other side of the Park for "the happiest cruise that ever sailed around the world."

It's A Small World, in Fantasyland, takes its passengers on a journey through six continents. Along the way, the children of more than 100 nations sing and dance and weave the magic spell that charmed more than 10 million people at the New York World's Fair in the mid-1960's.

The children, and children's toys, and toy-like animals, perform against the stylized, colorful background of familiar landmarks around the world. There are Danish castles and the onion-shaped pointed domes of Russia, Turkish mosques and Japanese arches, the glittering towers of Brazil's Rio, and bright-hued grassland huts of Africa. And there are the sometimes subtle, sometimes bold symbols: a Middle East sun, warmly feminine with eyelids demurely closed and long, flowing veil half hiding her face; or a giant sombrero shading dancers who perform the Mexican hat dance.

Costumed in the traditional festival-day outfits of their native lands, the children are brought to life through the electronic magic of *Audio-Animatronics.* From the first chorus to the final fling, the show is a merry fantasy of childhood symbolized in the words of the title tune: "Though the mountains divide and the oceans are wide, it's a small world. . .after all."

Tomorrowland II

Of all the changes in all the lands of Disneyland through the years, none has been more dramatic than the re-design and re-building of Tomorrowland. The biggest change came in 1967, but pencil first touched plan in 1955, when Walt Disney dedicated the first Tomorrowland with these descriptive words:

"Tomorrowland . . . A vista into a world of wondrous ideas, signifying man's achievement . . . a step into the future, with predictions of constructive things to come. Tomorrow offers new frontiers in science, adventure and ideals: the atomic age . . . and the hope for a peaceful and unified world."

To meet the challenge these words held out has meant a continuing pursuit of man's achievements on the new frontiers of science, adventure and ideals. For since the day in 1957 when Sputnik first rocketed skyward and rocked the world, man has pushed the frontiers back as never before. By the mid-1960's, the astronauts and cosmonauts, the men of science and the men of industry, had made the original To-morrowland area a "mock-one" edition of the future. The time for change had come.

We have already seen how the New York World's Fair came to influence all of Disneyland; first through the impetus it gave to the development of *Audio-Animatronics;* and second through the development of a new kind of relationship between Walt Disney and his creative staff at WED Enterprises on the one hand, and American industry on the other. No area so symbolizes that relationship as the $20 million To-morrowland that sprang up in 1967.

In an early statement expressing the idea for To-morrowland, Walt Disney had said: "The trip through 'space' will be scientifically correct. The roaring ride through the universe will depict the exploding stars, constellations, planets and comets exactly as charted, *and be no less thrilling for being authentic."*

The credo *authenticity* has governed the design and creation of all the attractions in Tomorrowland. Today, in Tomorrowland, the visitor can ride aboard an "Atomobile" into an *Adventure Thru Inner Space* (Monsanto). . . enjoy the sounds and words of songs that tell the story of our nation's growth ("America Sings") inside the world-famous Carousel Theatre, where the stages "stand still" and the audience rides

from act to act . . . feel the pull of gravity at "blast-off" on the *Mission to Mars* (McDonnell Douglas) . . . travel on the PeopleMover for a preview of tomorrow's transportation (Goodyear) . . . pause in a refreshment garden to dance to the music of popular bands at *Tomorrowland Terrace* (Coca-Cola). . . and visit *America the Beautiful* through the magic of the Circle-Vision 360 cameras (the Bell System).

Today's Tomorrowland also retains four of the most popular attractions from the past — the monorail, Submarine Voyage, Autopia freeways and the Skyway. One more, the racing Rocket Jets, has been re-designed and is now the centerpiece for Tomorrowland — a symbolic rocket reaching 80-feet into the sky, with whirling jets circling the pylon.

(One additional centerpiece in Tomorrowland is "the single most spectacular tree in all Disneyland," according to landscapers. A 19-trunk Senegal date palm, it has seen all the years of this century and more. Its age is estimated at more than 90.)

These attractions, in combination with its new adventures, have made Tomorrowland a *world on the move*. The best way to see it all is to board the *People-Mover*. The trip begins along the mall that marks

Tomorrowland's entryway, then ducks inside the buildings for previews of shows presented by some of America's major companies. Outside once more, the PeopleMover becomes a "highway in the sky," traveling *over* the Skyway and above the Autopia Freeways.

At Disneyland, the PeopleMover combines a preview and demonstration of its broader transportation potential, with a dash of showmanship. It's a "thrill," for example, to see the water falling away below as your PeopleMover car glides soundlessly above the tumbling waterfalls of the Submarine Voyage. And as the narrator points out when the PeopleMover passes through the Character Shop (a Disney-themed toy

and merchandise mart), this is "the modern way to window shop."

Like the monorail before it, Tomorrowland's PeopleMover demonstrates the potential of a unique transportation system. But where monorail was an old idea in a new showcase, the PeopleMover is a new concept developed by Disney engineers and introduced for the first time, anywhere, in Tomorrowland.

The PeopleMover is a silent, all-electric system that need never stop running. The cars continue to move even while passengers step aboard or disembark, for the loading-unloading platform moves too, at the same speed as the PeopleMover cars. The effect

Mammoth dinosaurs who once roamed the North American continent clash in "The Primeval World."

is almost as simple as stepping into a parked car in your own driveway.

From a community transit point of view, the distinguishing feature of the PeopleMover is its independent drive system. Power is supplied from a series of motors embedded in the track, completely separate from the cars. The result is that individual motors may cease to function without affecting the operation of the entire system. In city use, no single car could break down and cause a rush hour traffic jam.

Another unusual vehicle, called an "Atomobile," carries guests on a science-factual trip designed to communicate a complex idea while entertaining an audience. *Adventure thru Inner Space* is a journey deep into the realm of the atom and the molecule. Aboard the two-passenger Atomobiles, guests travel through the huge "Mighty Microscope," which is focused on a snowflake. Mysteriously, passengers appear to "shrink" as they emerge from the microscope, and enter a world where the delicate snowflake has become a towering wall of ice.

As the journey progresses, passengers continue to "grow smaller" within a world of giant crystals, mammoth water molecules, and finally the atom itself. Like streaking comets, electrons whirl wildly around the Atomobiles. Moments later, all is serene as the cars pierce the wall of the oxygen atom, and glide silently past the glowing nucleus of the atom in the quiet vastness of inner space.

Today man reaches for the stars. But as Adventure thru Inner Space seeks to dramatize, there is still another world awaiting exploration and scientific conquest. It is the world of the microscope, a kingdom that has seldom been portrayed to mass audiences in so exciting a way as it is in Tomorrowland.

From inner space to outer space is just a matter of moments in Tomorrowland. Perhaps the most symbolic of all its adventures is the *Mission to Mars,* which updated and replaced the simulated *Flight to the Moon* in 1975.

The journey begins in Mission Control — a simulated operations center where all activities at a spaceport of the future are being monitored by an eight-man crew and its flight director (*Audio-Animatronics* again).

In this three-ring circus of the space age, there are flashing panels of red, green and yellow lights, and eight television-size monitors picturing activities taking place on the base and out in space. Overhead are eight more small motion picture screens, and a large central screen on which the flight director "calls out" (selects) individual pictures for special attention.

The factual description of "base operations" and "space operations" by Mission Control's animated director is accompanied by extraordinary film of space flight activities. Among the highlights are views of America's astronauts working and performing zero-gravity acrobatics aboard Skylab. Finally, "Mars Spaceliner Flight 292" — your flight — is ready to depart, and moments later you are seated aboard the rocket ship itself, ready for blast-off.

Mermaids and sunken treasure are viewed through underwater portholes in the Submarine Voyage.

51

Explorer canoes and the sailing ship Columbia cruise the Frontierland river.

The Mars Spaceliner carries 162 passengers on its "Mission" to the red planet in distant space. Photos transmitted over thousands of miles from deep space by the Mariner flights have given scientists a detailed concept of Mars' surface; during this futuristic flight, passengers see and experience close-up views of enormous peaks and valleys and canyons on Mars, including one that truly dwarfs America's Grand Canyon in size.

There's also a short "in-flight" film titled "Mad Mars Myths" reviewing some of the wild ideas Earth-

Geppetto's Village nestles beneath the Swiss Alps in miniaturized Storybook Land.

man has imagined about life on Mars. But aside from this touch of the imaginary, the "fantastic" is really the trip itself — a science-possible space adventure of the future . . . a future that may not be as far away as it may seem when we remember that man's first space orbit of the Earth came in the 1960's.

There's one Tomorrowland show where the audience doesn't travel at all. Instead, the pageantry of *America the Beautiful* comes right to you . . . *all around you,* in fact, inside the Circle-Vision 360 theatre.

This is the newest of Circle-Vision shows, a panoramic and pageant-filled tour of America from sea to shining sea — and beyond the continental United States to Alaska and Hawaii. In the telling, far more than America's beauty unfolds. Surrounding the audience in the Circle-Vision theatre are the homes of presidents, from Washington's Mount Vernon to Lincoln's New Salem; the legendary frontiers, from the cattle country of the Great Southwest to Alaska's "land of the midnight sun"; man-made wonders, from the Statue of Liberty to the Golden Gate; and finally, the Pacific paradise, Hawaii, with its majestic Diamond Head and sparkling Waikiki Beach.

In the years since it was first introduced at Disneyland in 1955, Circle-Vision has circled the globe. There are few ways as dramatic and inspiring to visit *America the Beautiful* than to find it all around you as Circle-Vision's multiple cameras soar over Mt. Rushmore, sail the waters of California's Balboa Bay, and see the quiet village greens and traditional covered bridges of old New England.

The grandeur of the Grand Canyon is viewed from trains of the Disneyland Railroad.

The Haunted Mansion

For years, the house had stood unoccupied. Only a small sign offered a clue about what might be happening within.

"Notice!," it screamed. "All Ghosts and Restless Spirits . . . post-lifetime leases are now available in this HAUNTED MANSION! Don't be left out in the sunshine. Enjoy *active retirement* in this country club atmosphere — the fashionable address for famous ghosts, ghosts trying to make a name for themselves . . . and ghosts afraid to live by themselves! Leases include License to scare the daylights out of guests visiting these happy haunting grounds. For reservations, send resume of past experience to: Ghost Relations Dept., Disneyland.

"Please! Do not apply in person!"

And soon the letters came, from many parts of the world. There was the nine-year-old who wrote, "On Halloween I help in a spook house at our school," and the 12-year-old who claimed to have "scared my mom clear out of her wits." And the frustrated New England spinster, chagrined because "not a one of my neighbors believe in witches . . . *anymore.*"

The long-awaited Haunted Mansion opened its creaking doors in 1969, along the banks of Disneyland's muddy Mississippi, the Rivers of America. Situated on the edge of New Orleans Square, it proudly boasts of its distinguished residents, literally gathered over the years through the world-wide "talent hunt" . . . and the application of all the Disney skills of illusion and the dimensional arts of animation. (One group of special effects experts at WED Enterprises, charged with making "ghosts" appear and disappear on demand, proudly hung out a new shingle on their door: "Illusioneering Department.")

Filled with 999 ghosts and goblins and ghouls, Disneyland's Haunted Mansion is pleased to offer its guests an opportunity . . . to become number 1,000. All the spirits are "just dying to meet you" as you ride aboard a *Doom Buggy* through the seance room

In the shadow of the Matterhorn Mountain, submarines glide beneath the sea, and monorail trains cruise over the "highway in the sky" in Tomorrowland.

to meet the infamous Madame Leota . . . the corridor of haunted portraits that change from new to aged at the flash of a lightning bolt . . . and the Grand Hall where guests are arriving for dinner and dancing to the haunting strains of a thunderous organ recital — played by a see-through organist. And for those who think of graveyards as lonely, mysterious, eerie . . . there's the wildest scene of all: a singing, swinging playground for ghosts of all sizes, shapes and talents.

There are sights and sounds within this Haunted Mansion that few will ever forget. As your Ghost Host whispers with pride: "When hinges creak in doorless chambers and strange and frightening sounds echo through the halls . . . Whenever candlelights flicker where the air is deathly still . . . *that* is the time that ghosts are present, practicing their terror with ghoulish delight."

Bear Country

It was a spring day in 1966. With several new projects on the drawing boards, including the enormous Walt Disney World in Florida, Walt Disney had begun a typical process — tossing out an idea here, a concept there, to see what would "grow."

"Why don't we try something with *bears?*" Walt suggested to several designers and story men. Bears?

"Yea, a bear band, you know, to play music and things . . ."

Almost six years later, *Country Bear Jamboree* opened an extended run in Disneyland. Time and song and story had shaped their personalities, and now there they were on stage — Zeke and Zeb, Ted and Fred and the other fugitives from hibernation Walt had foreseen, playing "music and things."

Country Bear Jamboree is the hit show of Disneyland's seventh land, the wilderness land of *Bear Country*. Set in the great Northwoods of the latter 1800's, Bear Country is just down river from Frontierland, around the bend from New Orleans Square. A forest of tall pine shades the area, and a rushing mountain

stream flows right through town. Across the trestle, high overhead, trains of the Disneyland railroad roll by, "getting up steam" as they head out into the *real* wilderness.

In Bear Country, there's a soft drink "bar" called the Mile Long Bar because it looks . . . a mile long. You can spin the wheel of fortune at Teddi Barra's Swingin' Arcade, or search for out-of-the-ordinary items at Ursus J. Bear's Wilderness Outpost and the Indian Trading Post. Down at the landing, you can climb aboard an Explorer's Canoe to paddle 'round the Rivers of America. And you can dine on the porch of the Hungry Bear Restaurant overlooking the river, imagining another time and other places in a world that lives again . . . if only during dinner.

But to really know Bear Country is to step inside the mine tunnel that leads to the Country Bear Jamboree . . . "the wildest show in the wilderness." A vaudeville-style free-for-all, the show is the newest wonder of the Audio-Animatronics system . . . a wild and wooly mixture of country music, comedy and corn.

The stars of the show are "just one big happy family," in the words of the master of ceremonies, Henry. There's Trixie, "a little bit of cuddlesome fluff," singing her sad lament, "Tears Will Be the Chaser for My Wine." There's Liverlips McGrowl, Wendall, and Terrance — the vibrating wreck from Nashville Tech, who shakes, rattles and rolls his bluegrass favorites. There's Gomer, dedicated wizard of the piano keyboard. And the Five Bear Rugs playing guitar, fiddle, mouth harp . . . and dishpan, corn jug and washboard. And the Sun Bonnets — Bunny, Bubbles and Beulah — three little pixies bemoaning their romantic mishaps.

But the real show-stoppers are three of the most astounding personalities ever to go before the footlights in any theatre, anywhere. From smallest to largest, start with Sammy, disguised as a coon-skin hat — worn by Henry. Sammy comes to life just in time to join Henry in a chorus of "Davy Crockett." And there's the cast's "big time swinger," Teddi

Stars of the Country Bear Jamboree include (top) Henry and mandolin-playing Wendall; guitar-strumming Big Al; and lovely Trixie, the "Tampa Temptation."

Barra — the delightful, delicate, dedicated and dimpled darling from the Dakotas. When Teddi comes swingin' down out of the rafters singin' "Heart We Did All That We Could," it's all Henry and the boys can do to stay put on stage. And finally, there's Big Al himself, back again for his tenth farewell performance . . . and probably, at long last, his last. By the time he rolls his eyes, flaps his jaw, and begins to croon his hillbilly rendition of "Blood on the Saddle," it's almost unbearable.

Perhaps more than any other Audio-Animatronics show at Disneyland, Country Bear Jamboree is a complete theatrical performance. It relies on creating the personalities of its cast almost instantly, precision timing, spoken comedy lines and humorous song lyrics. It is, in short, that rare combination in any theatre: a fast-paced, funny performance that leaves you wanting more when the curtains close.

The Disneyland Parades

Everyone loves a parade. At Disneyland, the love affair with marching bands, colorful "floats", mechanized marvels and breathtaking costumes began on the day of its dedication in 1955. Perhaps no street in America has seen more costumes, brass bands, stars and performers "on parade" than Main Street U.S.A. at Disneyland — including New York's Fifth Ave. and the "boulevard of the stars", Hollywood Blvd. in Los Angeles.

Everyday there's at least one parade at Disneyland. Sometimes it's only the 18-piece Disneyland Band marching down the avenue. Often it's a college or high school band from almost anywhere in America; literally hundreds perform here every year. But on the day you visit Disneyland, the parade is just as likely to be so "different" it may truly be called *unique* to the Magic Kingdom.

Disneyland has always had a Christmastime holiday parade. Over the years it came to be more and more a holiday season "performance" — the staging of a singing, dancing musical show moving up and down Main Street and often through other areas of Disneyland as well. The quintessence of this parade is called *Fantasy on Parade.*

In the evolution of Disneyland pageants, *The Main Street Electrical Parade* also deserves a special place . . . for it was a new dimension, even for Disneyland. It was staged in the early 1970's and more than likely will return one day in the future. More than half-a-million tiny, colorful lights were used, winking and twinkling in familiar forms and patterns — huge scenes and figures from Disney films, all "on parade." There were giraffes and hippos and Cinderella's pumpkin coach; scenes and characters from *Alice in Wonderland, Snow White and the Seven Dwarfs, Winnie the Pooh* and *Pinocchio;* a whole *Dumbo* circus in lights; and many more than 100 human performers too — all appropriately costumed and some even lighted. The individual parade units measured up to 14 feet in height and 75 feet in length, and all carried their own battery power and sound — synchronized in meter and rhythm from the floats themselves, not from loudspeakers along the parade route.

The *Main Street Electrical Parade* did not lose its popularity with Disneyland guests. But in the true Walt Disney tradition it went "on vacation" in favor of a better idea. That concept was *America on Parade.*

Perhaps no parade anywhere, anytime was more ambitious in what it set out to do than *America on Parade.* For at its heart, in a 35-minute performance, is the heartbeat of America — its past, its people, its ideals and its innovations. Conceived as a salute and celebration honoring the American Bicentennial, *America on Parade* began its *every day* performance in June, 1975 both at Disneyland and in Walt Disney World, Florida. In all, after its final march down Main Street and through these Magic Kingdoms in September of 1976, it had completed more than 1200 performances and entertained more than 25 *million* in-person guests.

A stylized, whimsical, animated look at America, its parade units were huge in size, yet toy-like in appearance. More than 50 parade units presented beloved pastimes and ways-of-life, important American creations and contributions to our civilization, and memorable moments in our history. A new family of Disney characters, the larger-than-life "People of America", towering nearly eight feet in height, seemed almost doll-like in appearance when measured against the height of Main Street buildings and the 20-foot high parade units. These motorized "sets" were the stages around which the costumed "dolls" would dance and skip, walk and talk.

The musical accent for this "great American happening" was also unique. The basic sound was the "Great American Band Organ." To this was added the effects of the MOOG Synthesizer. To create the total environment of sound that surrounds the audience at all times throughout the production, the basic theme music of *America on Parade* was "broadcast" to locations along the route, while other special production musical selections were "broadcast" to the various individual units themselves. Thus, the music of America — from "Yankee Doodle" to "Dixie" to "Sidewalks of New York" to "There's No Business Like Show Business" to "School Days" to "God Bless America" . . . became the enveloping fabric to knit this unique pageant together.

With specially-created fireworks accompanying each performance, the finale of each *America on Parade* was not only a spine-tingling moment . . . but the frosting on a 200th Birthday cake for the U.S.A. that made the minds-eye "old-fashioned 4th of July" literally an old-fashioned celebration.

"The Pirates of the Caribbean" burn and sack a port city.

Kings are Commoners
and Commoners are Kings

"The last time I saw Disneyland was something like a million miles ago," travel editor Jerry Hulse wrote in the Los Angeles *Times*. "It was July 18, 1955, and I was assigned to cover the opening.

"It was one of those hot July days, the day Disneyland was born. The happy world of wonders within a troubled world came to life when Walt Disney stepped off the Santa Fe and Disneyland train.

"Since that opening day, Disneyland has played host to U.S. presidents, kings and queens. But mostly it has been a place where ordinary people come to turn away from the world of atoms to enter a world of pleasure — a happy world where every adventure has a happy ending."

Disneyland has been called "a land where kings are commoners and commoners are kings." The description is explained in part by the long list of VIP's who have left their own kingdoms to visit this happy kingdom. There have been heads of royal families — His Majesty Mohammed V of Morocco, King Hussein of Jordan, Belgium's King Baudouin, King Bhumibol and Queen Sirikit of Thailand, Afghanistan's King Mohammed Zaher and Queen Homaira, King Mahendra and Queen Ratna of Nepal, and Denmark's King Frederick IX and Queen Ingrid. There have been presidents — Sukarno and Soeharto of Indonesia, Sekou Toure of Guinea, Abboud of the Sudan, Radhakrishnan of India, Estensorro of Bolivia, Yame-ogo of Upper Volta, Sunay of Turkey, Mobutu of the Congo Republic, Ceausescu of Romania and Truman, Eisenhower, Kennedy and Nixon of the U.S.A. (although none of the four was president at the time of his visit). There have been prime ministers — Suhrawardy of Pakistan, Mohammed Daud of Afghanistan, Nehru of India, Burnham of Guyana, Kittikachorn of Thailand. And there have been emperors

"America Sings" in Tomorrowland's Carousel Theatre — from "Down by the Riverside" to "Rock Around the Clock." More than 100 characters perform.

68

Architectural styles around the world are combined outside "It's A Small World."

(Haile Selassie of Ethiopia), numerous princes and princesses (including Prince Ranier of Monaco, and Crown Prince Akihito and Princess Michiko of Japan), and the Shah and Empress of Iran.

It is safe to say that today, the magic of the name Disney and the magnet of the place Disneyland stretches across America and reaches all around the world. There was the incident in the San Antonio, Texas, courtroom, for example. A prospective juror told the learned judge that he was perfectly willing to serve, but he had already made plans to take his six children to Disneyland. Noting that he had "made a similar commitment for this year," the judge ruled

without hesitation: juror excused.

And there was the editorial in the Louisville (Kentucky) *Courier-Journal:* "Foreign tourists should not be frightened away by reports of excessive red tape in the United States. It is not true, for example, that a separate visa is required for Disneyland."

But the fundamental reason for the king-commoner analogy is found in the basic approach to entertaining its guests that is practiced at Disneyland. Here hosts and hostesses strive to live up to a credo contained in the training manual at the University of Disneyland, a real classroom school that all who work here attend: "We love to entertain kings and queens,

Countries and children on every continent greet guests who sail through "It's A Small World."

but the vital thing to remember is this — *every* guest receives the VIP treatment."

Appropriately entitled, "You're on Stage at Disneyland," the training booklet sets forth a number of Disney trademarks:

"It's not just important to be friendly and courteous to the public, it's essential . . .

" 'Customer' is a bad word.

"We are hosts and hostesses, and *everyone* who enters our main gate is a guest."

Some visitors, however, have had difficulty being just plain guests, like everyone else. Everywhere motion picture star Betty Hutton went in Disneyland, other visitors recognized her and asked for autographs. So Miss Hutton determined to disguise herself. Spying Merlin's Magic Shop in Fantasyland, she purchased a clever concealment — long, false eyelashes, a buccaneer's hat and a special "sword" that appeared to go right through her head. The disguise worked perfectly; no one recognized Miss Hutton. But people continued to stop her. This time they weren't interested in autographs — they simply wanted to know where they could buy "a hat like that crazy one you've got on!"

What Is Not Yet Done

More than a century ago, the famous French author Alexis de Tocqueville heard the heartbeat of a new nation.

"America is a land of wonders," he wrote, "in which everything is in constant motion, and every change seems an improvement. No natural boundary seems to be set to the efforts of man; and in his eyes what is not yet done is only what he has not yet attempted to do."

What de Tocqueville wrote about America a hundred years ago could easily be said of Disneyland today. As Walt Disney said:

"I believe the fun is in building something, in bringing new things to life. We never do the same thing twice. After we've finished a job around here we head in another direction. We're always opening up new doors."

And in the months and years to come, the staff Walt Disney gathered together to plan, design and operate Disneyland will open wider the "new door" Walt had begun in central Florida. "In Florida," Walt Disney had said, "we have something special we never enjoyed at Disneyland — the blessing of size. There's enough land here to hold all the ideas and plans we can possibly imagine . . ."

In October, 1971, WALT DISNEY WORLD *opened to an eager public. Fifteen miles southwest of Orlando, in the lake and forest country of central Florida, Walt Disney World is a new kind of entertainment and recreation experience —* The Vacation Kingdom of the World. *Today a visit here is a voyage to many lands and times. Stroll through the* Magic Kingdom, *where — like Disneyland — the worlds of fantasy, yesterday and tomorrow "come to life" in thematic lands. Join the luau under the palms of the* Polynesian Village *resort-hotel. Ride a swift monorail train to the* Contemporary Resort — *as contemporary as tomorrow. Follow the trail to the* Fort Wilderness *campgrounds, nestled among the tall cypress and pine. You can visit here for the day, or better yet, plan to* stay *for an entire vacation . . . there's a holiday-full of things to do and places to go, all together for the first time in The Vacation Kingdom of the World.*

Writing in The Architectural Forum *magazine, Editor Peter Blake captured the spirit and promise of this "new world."*

"In a great many respects," Blake said, "the most interesting New Town in the U.S. is Walt Disney World. It is interesting not only because it is huge — 27,000 acres, or twice the size of Manhattan . . . or because it is so well financed ($400 million invested to date . . .); or because it is so unabashedly corny (i.e., such really enormous fun). It is interesting also, or even primarily, for what it can teach every architect, planner, and urban designer about any number of things that may have escaped his or her attention in the past."

The people who run Walt Disney World, Blake wrote, "think they have built and are building the nicest Fun City to date, and they are absolutely right. But they have done a great deal more than produce a Super Amusement Park, and this story is an attempt to look behind the masks and the fun of Mickey Mouse Land, and to find out what all of us can learn from the century's greatest showman and pop artist.

"For the man who did seem to know exactly what he was doing down there in that swamp near Orlando was the late Walt Disney himself . . ."

"You hate to repeat yourself," Walt Disney said. "I don't like to make sequels to my pictures. I like to take a new thing and develop something . . . a new concept."